W9-BFW-152

Dedication

.:.

First and foremost, thanks must go to Neil,
as always, friend and a half, and not a bad-looking gent,
writes a bit, I'm told.

To the three graces, Diana, Shelly, and Renae.
They have all, in one way or another,
made a great job an absolute delight.

To BWS, who's saved me from myself, twice.

This book is for you.

.:.

Michael Zulli,
in New England.
In a tower.
On a cliff.
By a river.

The Price

Tramps and vagabonds have marks they make on gateposts and trees and doors, letting others of their kind know a little about the people who live at the houses and farms they pass on their travels.

I think cats must leave similar signs.

How else to explain the cats who turn up at our door through the year, hungry and flea-ridden and abandoned?

We
take
them
in.

We get rid of the fleas and the ticks, feed them and take them to the vet.

We pay for them to get their shots--

and, indignity upon indignity--

we have them neutered or spayed.

And they stay with us, for a few months, or for a year, or forever.

Most of them arrive in summer. We live in the country, just the right distance out of town for the city-dwellers to abandon their cats near us.

The cat population of my house is currently as follows: Zoe, a half-Siamese, former barn-kitten, very gentle, very quiet.

Hermione and Pod, tabby and black, respectively, the mad sisters who live in my attic office, and do not mingle.

Princess, the blue-eyed long-haired white cat, who lived wild in the woods for years before she gave up her wild ways for soft sofas and beds.

And, last but largest, Furball, Princess's cushion-like calico long-haired daughter, orange and black and white...

whom I discovered as a tiny kitten in our garage one day, strangled and almost dead, her head poked through an old badminton net...

and who surprised us all by not dying but instead growing up to be the best-natured cat I have ever encountered.

And then there is the black cat. Who has no other name than the Black Cat, and who turned up almost a month ago.

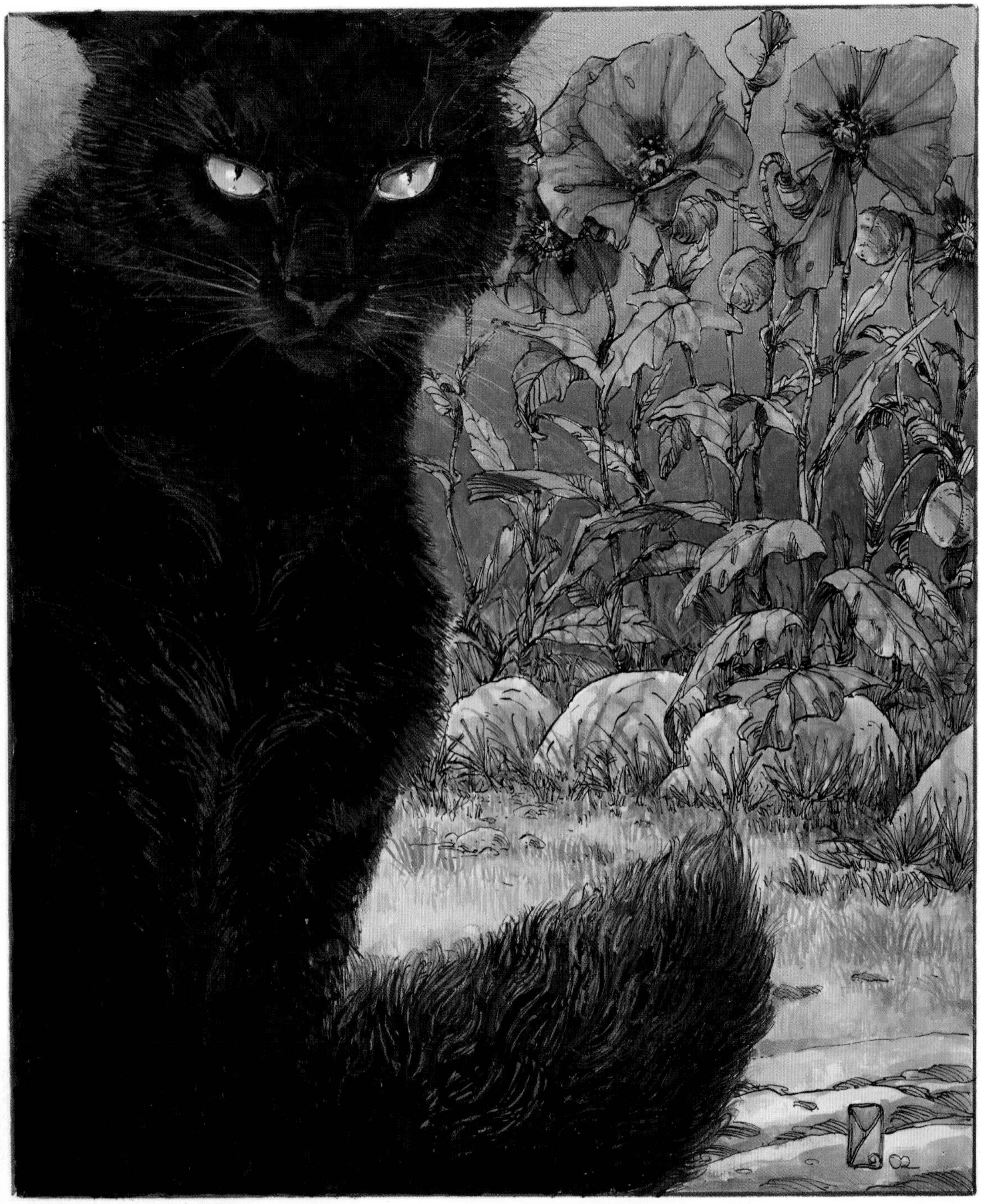

THE PRICE

We did not realize he was going to be living here at first: he looked too well-fed to be a stray, too old and jaunty to have been abandoned. He looked like a small panther, and he moved like a patch of night.

One day, in the summer, he was lurking about our ramshackle porch: eight or nine years old, at a guess, male, greenish-yellow of eye, very friendly, quite imperturbable.

I assumed he belonged to a neighboring farmer or household.

I went away for a few weeks, to finish writing a book, and when I came home he was still on our porch, living in an old cat-bed one of the children had found for him.

He was, however, almost unrecognizable. Patches of fur had gone, and there were deep scratches on his gray skin.

The tip of one ear was chewed away. There was a gash beneath one eye, a slice gone from one lip.

He looked tired and thin.

We took the Black Cat to the vet, where we got him some antibiotics, which we fed him each night, along with soft cat food.

We wondered who he was fighting. Princess, our white, beautiful, near-feral queen?

Raccoons? A rat-tailed, fanged possum?

Each night the scratches would be worse-- one night his side would be chewed up; the next, it would be his underbelly, raked with claw marks and bloody to the touch.

When it got to that point, I took him down to the basement to recover, beside the furnace and the piles of boxes.

He was surprisingly heavy, the Black Cat, and I picked him up and carried him down there, with a cat-basket, and a litter bin, and some food and water.

I closed the door behind me.

I had to wash the blood from my hands, when I left the basement.

He stayed down there for four days.

At first he seemed too weak to feed himself: a cut beneath one eye had rendered him almost one-eyed, and he limped and lolled weakly, thick yellow pus oozing from the cut in his lip.

I went down there every morning and every night, and I fed him, and gave him antibiotics, which I mixed with his canned food, and I dabbed at the worst of the cuts, and spoke to him.

He had diarrhea, and, although I changed his litter daily, the basement stank evilly.

The four days that the Black Cat lived in the basement were a bad four days in my house: the baby slipped in the bath, and banged her head, and might have drowned;

I learned that a project I had set my heart on--adapting Hope Mirrlees' novel *Lud-in-the-Mist* for the BBC--was no longer going to happen, and I realized that I did not have the energy to begin again from scratch, pitching it to other networks, or to other media;

my daughter left for summer camp, and immediately began to send home a plethora of heart-tearing letters and cards, five or six each day, imploring us to take her away; my son had some kind of fight with his best friend, to the point that they were no longer on speaking terms;

and returning home one night, my wife hit a deer, who ran out in front of the car. The deer was killed, the car was left undrivable, and my wife sustained a small cut over one eye.

By the fourth day, the cat was prowling the basement. He mewed at me to let him out, and, reluctantly, I did so.

He went back onto the porch, and slept there for the rest of the day.

The next morning there were deep, new gashes in his flanks, and clumps of black cat-hair--his-- covered the wooden boards of the porch.

Letters arrived that day from my daughter, telling us that camp was going better, and she thought she could survive a few days;

my son and his friend sorted out their problem, although what the argument was about--trading cards, computer games, *Star Wars*, or A Girl--I would never learn.

The BBC executive who had vetoed *Lud-in-the-Mist* was discovered to have been taking bribes (well, "question-able loans")

from an independent production company, and was sent home on permanent leave:

his successor, I was delighted to learn, when she faxed me, was the woman who had initially proposed the project to me before leaving the BBC.

I thought about returning the Black Cat to the basement, but decided against it. Instead, I resolved to try and discover what kind of animal was coming to our house each night, and from there to formulate a plan of action--to trap it, perhaps.

For birthdays and at Christmas my family gives me gadgets and gizmos, pricey toys which excite my fancy but, ultimately, rarely leave their boxes.

There's a food dehydrator and an electric carving knife, a bread-making machine, and, last year's present...

a pair of see-in-the-dark binoculars.

Perhaps, I thought, if the creature, dog or cat or raccoon or what-have-you, were to see me sitting on the porch, it would not come...

so I took a chair into the box-and-coat-room, little larger than a closet, which overlooks the porch,

and, when everyone in the house was asleep, I went out onto the porch, and bade the Black Cat good night.

That cat, my wife had said, when he first arrived, *is a person.*

And there was something very person-like in his huge, leonine face: his broad black nose, his greenish-yellow eyes, his fanged but amiable mouth (still leaking amber pus from the right lower lip).

I stroked his head, and scratched him beneath the chin, and I wished him well.

Then I went inside, and turned off the light on the porch.

I sat on my chair, in the darkness inside the house, with the see-in-the-dark binoculars on my lap. I had switched the binoculars on, and a trickle of greenish light came from the eyepieces.

Time passed, in the darkness.

I experimented with looking at the darkness with the binoculars, learning to focus, to see the world in shades of green.

I found myself horrified by the number of swarming insects I could see in the night air: it was as if the night world were some kind of nightmarish soup, swimming with life.

Then I lowered the binoculars from my eyes,

and stared out at the rich blacks and blues of the night, empty and peaceful and calm.

Time passed. I struggled to keep awake, found myself profoundly missing cigarettes and coffee, my two lost addictions. Either of them would have kept my eyes open.

But before I had tumbled too far into the world of sleep and dreams, a yowl from the garden jerked me fully awake.

I fumbled the binoculars to my eyes...

and was disappointed to see that it was merely Princess.

She vanished into the woodland to the right of the house, and was gone.

I was about to settle myself back down, when it occurred to me to wonder what exactly had startled Princess so.

I began scanning the middle distance with the binoculars, looking for a huge raccoon, a dog, or a vicious possum.

And there was indeed something coming down the driveway, towards the house.

I could see it through the binoculars, clear as day.

It was the Devil.

I had never seen the Devil before, and although I had written about him in the past, if pressed would have confessed that I had no belief in him, other than as an imaginary figure, tragic and Miltonian.

The figure coming up the driveway was not Milton's Lucifer. It was the Devil.

My heart began to pound in my chest, to pound so hard that it hurt. I hoped it could not see me, that, in a dark house, behind window glass, I was hidden.

The figure flickered and changed as it walked up the drive. One moment it was dark, bull-like, minotaurish, the next it was slim and female, and the next it was a cat itself, a scarred, huge gray-green wildcat, its face contorted with hate.

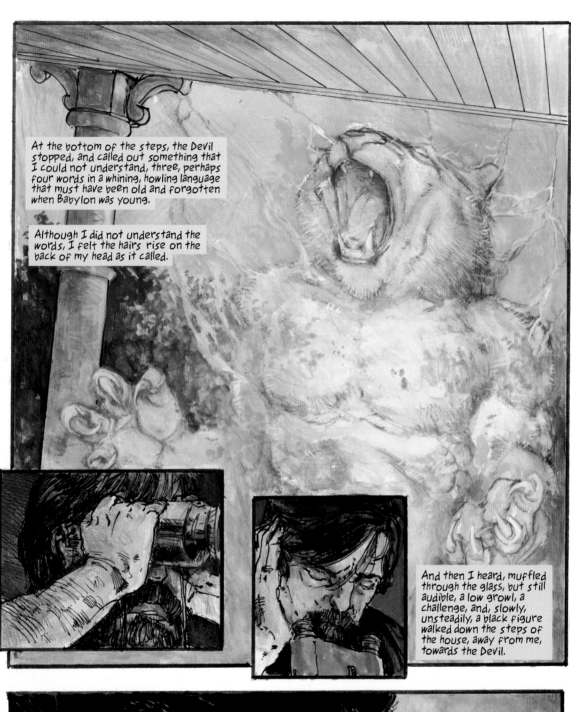

At the bottom of the steps, the Devil stopped, and called out something that I could not understand, three, perhaps four words in a whining, howling language that must have been old and forgotten when Babylon was young.

Although I did not understand the words, I felt the hairs rise on the back of my head as it called.

And then I heard, muffled through the glass, but still audible, a low growl, a challenge, and, slowly, unsteadily, a black figure walked down the steps of the house, away from me, towards the Devil.

These days the Black Cat no longer moved like a panther; instead he stumbled and rocked, like a sailor only recently returned to land.

The Devil was a woman, now.

She said something soothing and gentle to the cat, in a tongue that sounded like French, and reached out a hand to him.

He sank his teeth into her arm, and her lip curled, and she spat at him.

The woman glanced up at me, then, and if I had doubted that she was the Devil before, I was certain of it now:

the woman's eyes flashed red fire at me; but you can see no red through the night-vision binoculars, only shades of a green.

And the Devil saw me, through the window. It saw me. I am in no doubt about that at all.

The Devil twisted and writhed,

and now it was some kind of jackal, a flat-faced, huge-headed, bull-necked creature,

halfway between a hyena and a dingo.

There were maggots squirming in its mangy fur,

and it walked closer, approaching the steps.

Approaching my house.

The Black Cat leapt upon it,

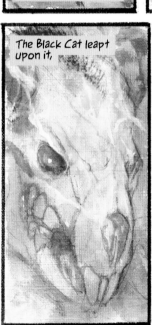

and in seconds they became a rolling, writhing thing,

moving faster than my eyes could follow.

All this in silence.

And then a low roar--down the country road at the bottom of our drive lumbered a late-night truck, its blazing headlights burning bright as green suns through the binoculars.

I lowered them from my eyes, and saw only darkness, and the gentle yellow of headlights, and then the red of rear lights as it vanished off again into the nowhere at all.

When I raised the binoculars once more, there was nothing to be seen. Only the Black Cat, on the steps, staring up into the air.

I trained the binoculars up, and saw something flying away--a Vulture, perhaps, or an eagle-- and then it flew beyond the trees and was gone.

I went out onto the porch, and picked up the Black Cat,

and stroked him, said kind, soothing things to him.

He mewled piteously when I first approached him, but, after a while, he went to sleep on my lap, and I put him into his basket, and went upstairs to my bed, to sleep myself.

There was dried blood on my T-shirt and jeans, the following morning.

That was a week ago.

The thing that comes to my house does not come every night. But it comes most nights: we know it by the wounds on the cat, and the pain I can see in those leonine eyes. He has lost the use of his front left paw, and his right eye has closed for good.

I wonder what we did to deserve the Black Cat.

I wonder who sent him...

And, selfish and scared, I wonder how much more he has to give.

END

The Daughter of Owls

AH.
WYLD. GOOD
EVENING.

EVENING,
AUBREY. YOU'RE
LATE.

SORRY,
OLD FELLOW. BEASTLY
WEATHER.

NOW, YOU SAID
YOU HAD A TALE FOR MY
COLLECTION...?

YES. YES, I
DO. I HEARD IT FROM
OLD FARRINGDON, WHO
SAID IT WAS AN OLD
STORY WHEN HE
HEARD IT.

SOUNDS
LIKE THE KIND
OF THING YOU WERE
LOOKING FOR. ALL
NONSENSE, OF
COURSE. BUT
STILL.

FARRINGDON
CALLED IT "THE
DAUGHTER OF
OWLS."

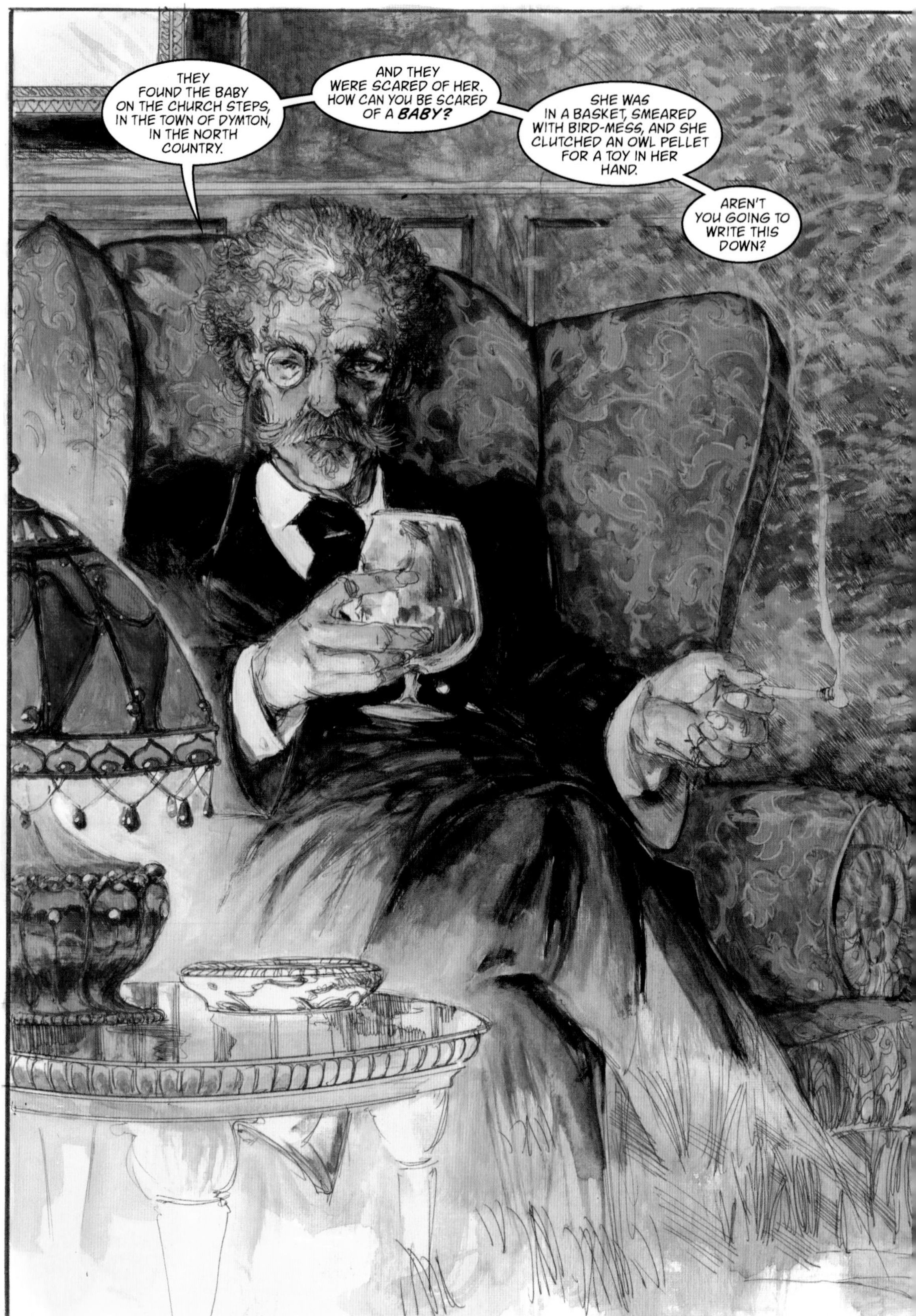
THEY FOUND THE BABY ON THE CHURCH STEPS, IN THE TOWN OF DYMTON, IN THE NORTH COUNTRY.
AND THEY WERE SCARED OF HER. HOW CAN YOU BE SCARED OF A *BABY?*
SHE WAS IN A BASKET, SMEARED WITH BIRD-MESS, AND SHE CLUTCHED AN OWL PELLET FOR A TOY IN HER HAND.
AREN'T YOU GOING TO WRITE THIS DOWN?

The Daughter of Owls

In the Town of Dymton a newborn girl was left one night on the steps of the Church...

The Sexton found her there the next morning, and she had hold of a curious thing...

i.e., the pellet of an Owl, which, when crumbled, showed the usual composition of an hoot-owl's pellet:

That is to say, it contained skin and teeth and small bones.

The women of the town talked amongst themselves, and the oldest of them said as follows:

That the girl was the daughter of owls, and that she should be burned to death, for she was not born of woman.

And the other wives of the town agreed that the baby should be put to death.

Notwithstanding this, wiser heads and graybeards prevailed.

The laws of the county and of the land were consulted, and a judgment was delivered.

And soon it was announced that the babe was not to be killed. Instead, she was to be taken to the old convent, several miles from the town, and there she was to remain.

She would remain behind the high stone walls...

babe and infant...

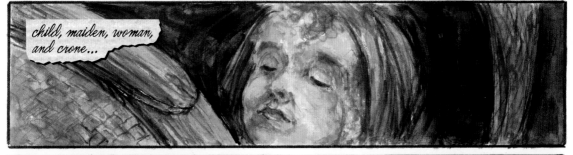

child, maiden, woman, and crone...

until she died.

Now, this was shortly after the Papish times, and the old convent had been left empty, for the Townsfolk thought it was a place of Devils and such.

Hoot-owls and Screech-owls and many bats made their homes in the tower.

There was no one living there, only one old woman, who had, long ago, been a nun...

and now was merely a crabbed old crone with nowhere else to go....

Who prayed night and day, and spoke to no one but her God.

It was at the convent that the babe was left, and the old woman who was no longer a nun agreed that she would feed it, although she would have no other contact with it, for it was a damned thing, and she was a holy woman.

And, although the
old woman had doubts,
she fed the babe faithfully...

once each morning and
once again each night...

Fed her on the thin gruel that, like the babe,
having no teeth, was all the crone could eat.

It was predicted, in the town, that the babe
would die, which
she did not do...

although, in time, the old woman went to
her reward, and left the child alone.

By the time that she was a maid of sixteen summers, she was the prettiest thing you ever did see.

Still, she spent her days and nights behind high stone walls, seeing no one, but only a townswoman who came at dusk to leave food.

One market day the good-wife talked too loudly of the girl's beauty...

And she said also that the girl could not speak, for having heard no human voices in her short life, she had never learned the manner of it.

The men of Dymton, the graybeards and the young men, were much taken with this, and they spoke to one another...

saying: "If we were to visit her, who would ever know?"

So the menfolk announced that they would go hunting all in a company, when the moon was full:

And on the night of the full moon, they went one by one from their houses...

The Reeve of Dymton unlocked the convent gate.

They found her hiding in the cellar, scared by the noise.

38

The maid was more pretty than even they had imagined.

When she saw them she was terrified. She had never seen a man before, only the women who brought her food.

She stared at them with huge eyes and she uttered small cries, as if she were imploring them not to hurt her.

The townsfolk merely laughed, for they were set on their evil mischief, and were wicked cruel men: and they came at her in the moon's light.

Then the girl began a-screeching and a-wailing, but that did not stay them from their purpose.

And the great window went dark, and the light of the moon was blocked.

And there was the sound of mighty wings; but the men did not see it as they were intent on their ravishment...

The women of Dymton, asleep in their beds that night, dreamed that they could hear hoots and screeches and howls.

They dreamed of gargantuan birds.

They dreamed that they were transformed into little mice and rats.

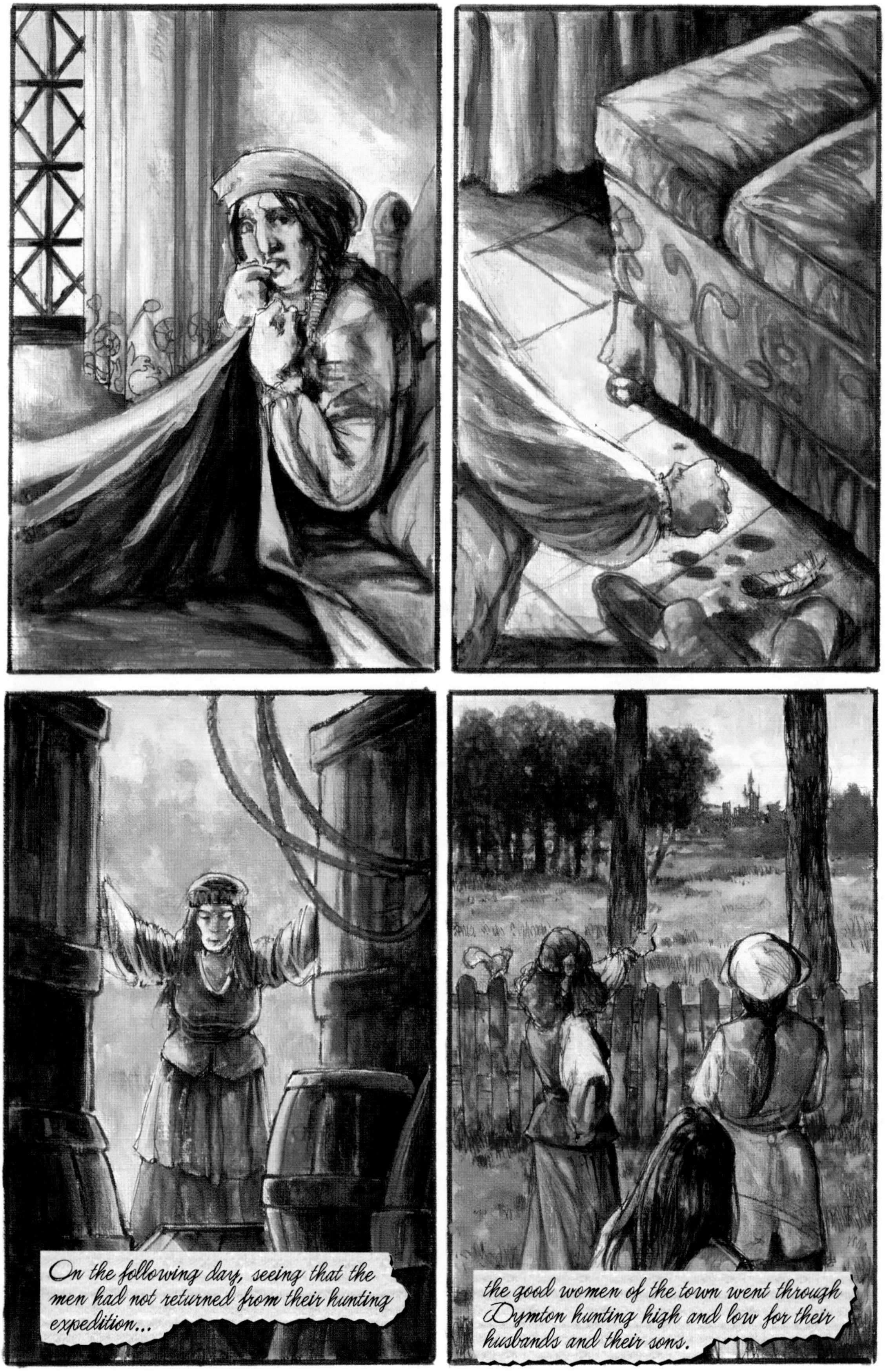
On the following day, seeing that the men had not returned from their hunting expedition...
the good women of the town went through Dymton hunting high and low for their husbands and their sons.

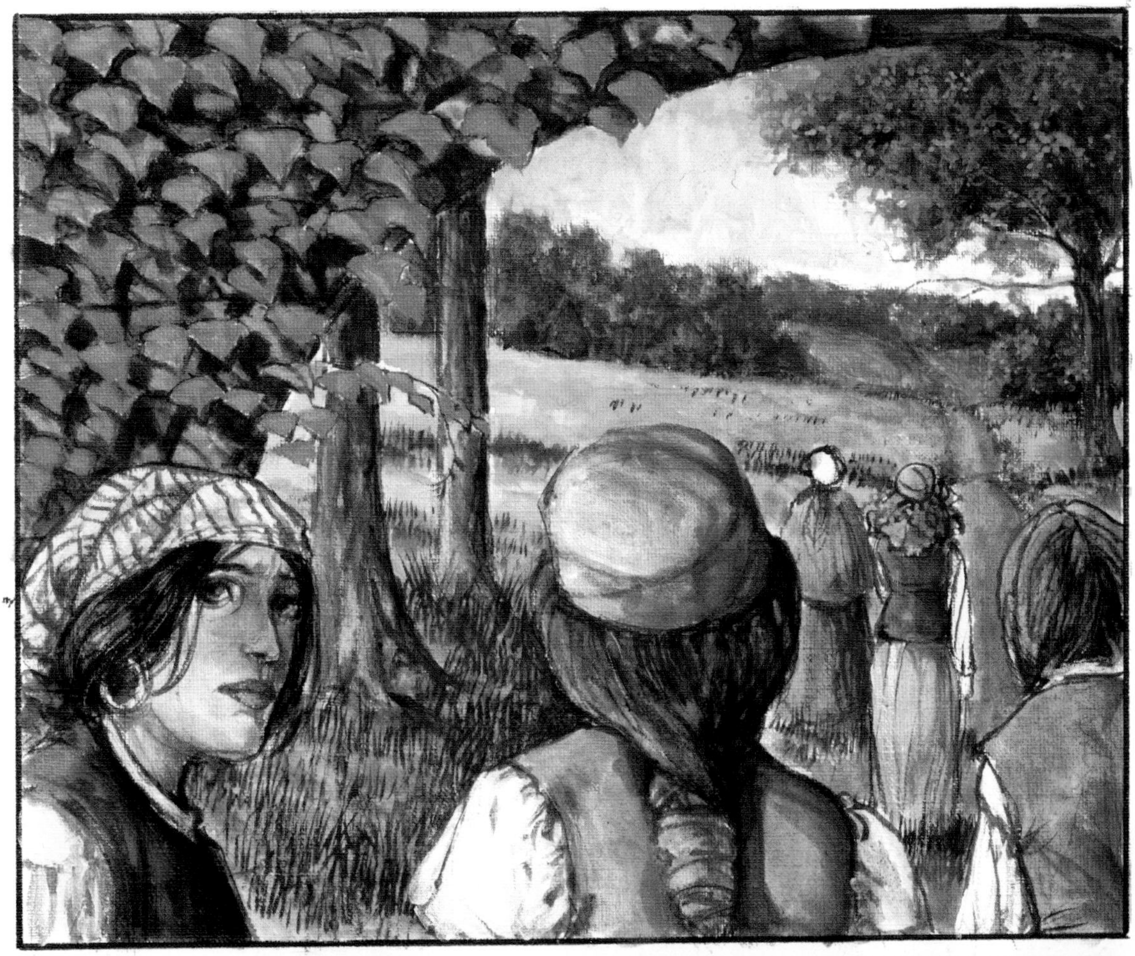

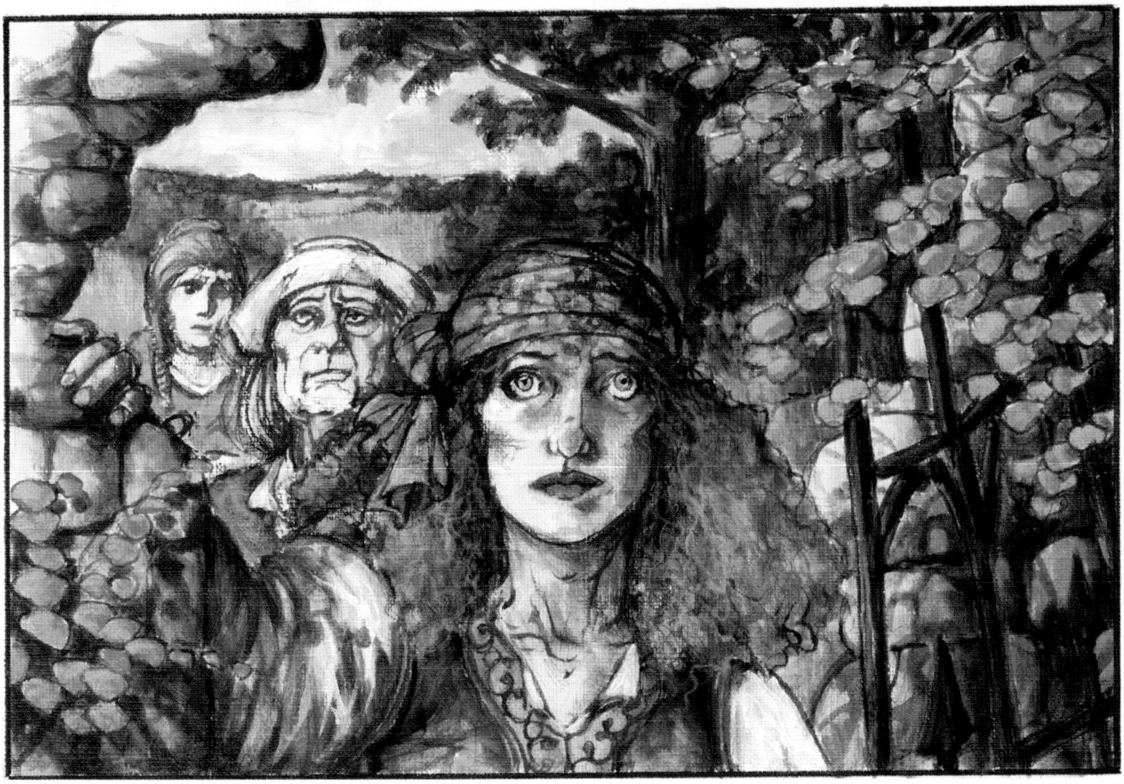

Eventually...

coming to the convent...

they found on the cellar stones...

the pellets of owls; and in the pellets they discovered hair and buckles and coins, and small bones; and also a quantity of straw upon the floor.

And the men of Dymton were none of them seen again.

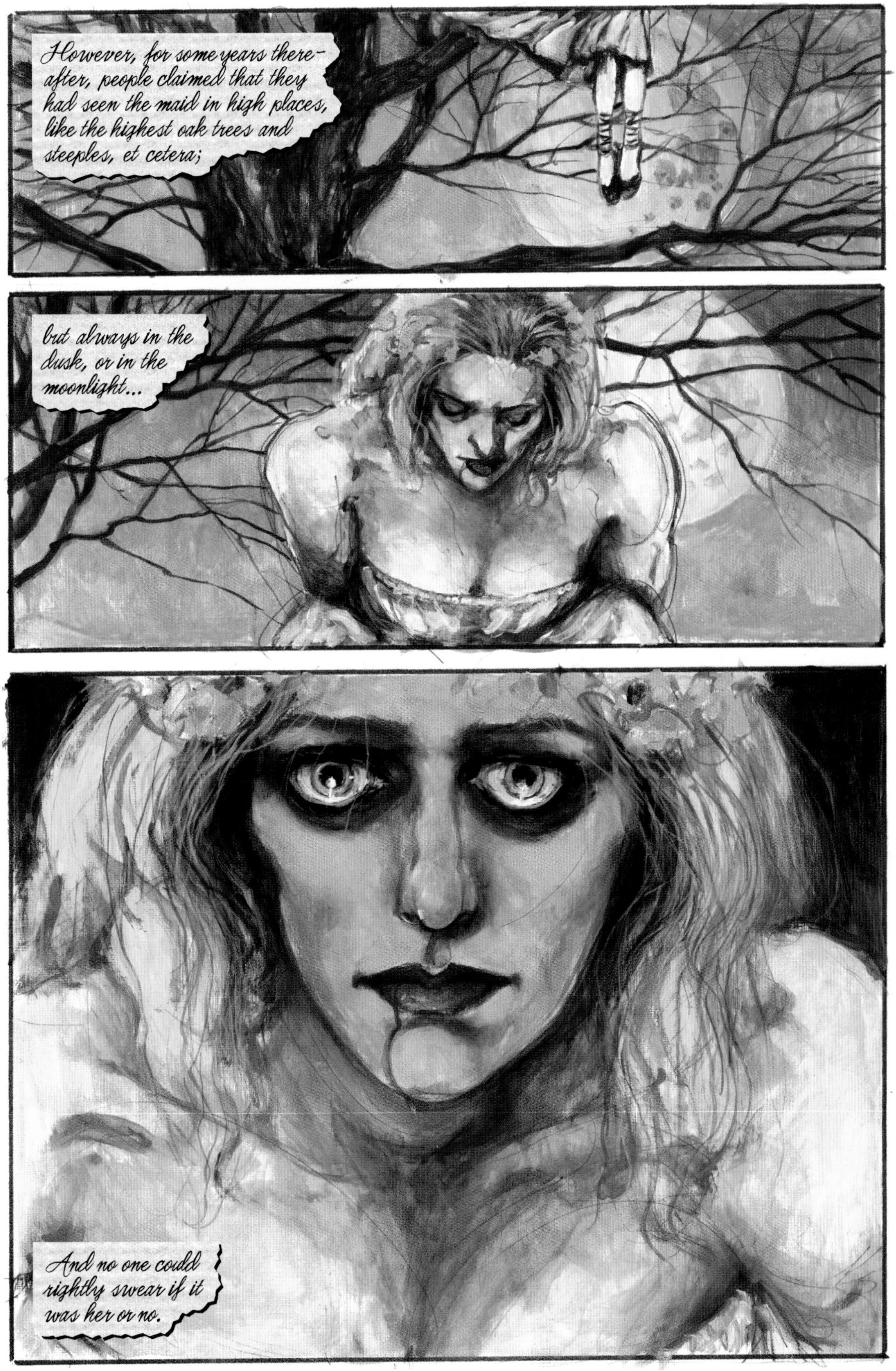
However, for some years there-after, people claimed that they had seen the maid in high places, like the highest oak trees and steeples, et cetera;
but always in the dusk, or in the moonlight...
And no one could rightly swear if it was her or no.

(She was a white figure-- but Mr. Edmund Wyld could not actually remember whether the folk who claimed to have seen her believed she wore clothes or was naked.)

The truth of it all is obvious, but it is a merry story and one which I write down here, to amuse my readers, and put them in mind of simpler times, when people believed such tales.

Aubrey Johns,
3rd February 1897

The End

❖

EDITOR
DIANA SCHUTZ

DESIGNER
LIA RIBACCHI

DIGITAL PRODUCTION
CHRIS HORN

PUBLISHER
MIKE RICHARDSON

❖❖

CREATURES OF THE NIGHT™

"The Price" ™ © 2004 Neil Gaiman. "The Daughter of Owls" ™ © 2004 Neil Gaiman. Artwork © 2004 Michael Zulli. Creatures of the Night is a trademark of Neil Gaiman. All rights reserved. No portion of this publication may be reproduced or transmitted, in any form or by any means, without the express written permission of the copyright holders. Names, characters, places, and incidents featured in this publication are either the product of the author's imagination or are used fictitiously. Any resemblance to actual persons [living or dead], events, institutions, or locales, without satiric intent, is coincidental. Dark Horse Books is a trademark of Dark Horse Comics, Inc. Dark Horse Comics® is a trademark of Dark Horse Comics, Inc., registered in various categories and countries. All rights reserved.

Published by
Dark Horse Books
A division of Dark Horse Comics, Inc.
10956 SE Main Street
Milwaukie, Oregon 97222

First edition: November 2004
ISBN 1-56971-936-5

1 3 5 7 9 10 8 6 4 2
PRINTED IN CHINA

❖

WITHDRAWN